SECRET WORK AT HOME RESOURCES

YOUR GUIDE TO FINDING EMPLOYMENT FROM HOME

By

BK RICH

Copyright © 2015

www.BKRich.com

INTRODUCTION

Top Secret Work at Home Resources revealed!

Are you new to trying to find work from home? Been scammed by online job ads where you had to pay money to work? Well, this is your last stop! I'll give you a quick run down on my 17 years of telecommuting or working at home experience. Inside you'll find links to the top websites and forums to find legit work at home jobs with Fortune 500 Companies. However, it's up to you to do your due diligence.

TABLE OF CONTENTS

Introduction

Table of Contents

Legal Notes

Chapter 1. About Me

Chapter 2. Checklist

Chapter 3. Home Office Set Up

Chapter 4. The Resources (The Gold)

Chapter 5. Additional Tips

About The Author

Other Books By (Author)

Legal Notes

All rights reserved.

Disclaimer: This site is operated by BK Rich and its affiliated entities. The material contained herein is provided for informational purposes only. BK Rich does not claim that anyone purchasing this mini ebook will obtain employment. The information within this ebook are provided without warranties of any kind, either expressed or implied, including but not limited to warranties regarding the accuracy or completeness of the information contained on this site or in any referenced links. BK Rich reserves the right to make changes to this site at any time and without notice, and makes no commitment to update this site. Purchasing this e book implies that you understand you are purchasing information via "digital download" and once downloaded you are not entitled to a refund. ISP addresses are tracked.

Disclosure of Material Connection: Some of the links in this ebook/ report are "affiliate links." This means if you click on the link and purchase the item, I will receive an affiliate commission. Regardless, I only recommend products or services I use personally and believe will add value to my readers. I am disclosing this in accordance with the Federal Trade Commission's 16 CFR, Part 255: "Guides Concerning the Use of Endorsements and Testimonials in Advertising."

For more information, contact me at: 252-631-0127 or BKRichAssociates@gmail.com

CHAPTER 1. ABOUT ME

My name is Beverly better known as an "Internet Sleuth" or "Web Head" because for 17 years I have ferreted out coveted information regarding work at home freelance gigs, full and part time contract employment and employee type of employment. So yes, I've telecommuted or worked from the comfort of my home since 1998. Working all sorts of odd jobs online, everything from being the Director of Client Relations for a NY Music School, to web design, SEO, business consulting in which I co wrote a business plan that netted the company a 3 million dollar loan to data entry, sales, tech supervisor, recruiting, staffing, HR, marketing, customer service, mortgage and insurance telemarketing... you name it and I think I've done it in these last 17 yrs. And did it while raising a family.

Working in this manner has pretty much granted me the financial security and allowed me the freedom to move about, travel, spend more time with family and enjoy life more due to the fact that with most of my jobs are "telecommute". All I need or needed was an internet connection and a phone.

What I am about to reveal is more or less considered coveted or "Top Secret" information!Why is it coveted? Because the competition for work at home placement is unusually stiff these days. You have to be on top of your game to land "great" work at home jobs. However with these resources, you'll have access to insider info that will give you a leg up on where to start, what to look for and how to go about applying for employment.

These are the top secret, most coveted resources on the internet! These aren't easily found online and with ALL the online scams, it's difficult to sometimes tell which opportunities are legit from those that aren't. BUT now "YOU" have access to ALL the info you need to successfully find legit employment within the comfort of your home.

Is this going to be a drop in the bucket so to speak? Erm, nope! You have to do your own due diligence. You'll notice with the links below and the info you read on different companies, that not everyone will have the same experience. Your mileage will vary too. And the reason I'm even sharing why your mileage may vary is because of my experience in 2008 with a 3 yr old company who most everyone on the forums were screaming to stay away from. I was able to land an 18 month, 1600.00 bi-weekly salaried position with that company. Yes, they paid me on time every pay period. So with that, if you're interested in a straight commissioned part time outbound B2B phone sales position, by all means, email me at creativetelecommuter@gmail.com :-)! Be sure and enter "EMPLOY" in the subject line.

Now to the nitty gritty- The Resources, the real reason why you purchased my lil Ebook!

CHAPTER 2. CHECKLIST

(What you should have in place)

A. First things first! Please follow this checklist prior to joining any forums or applying for employment….

1. Set up a free Gmail email account just for the work at home forums and for applying for employment.

2. Set up a free Google Voice Phone Account for resume use and to protect your real home number till you find legit employment.

3. Update your resume and cover letter with your new gmail email address and your new google voice phone number. You can create an awesome professional looking resume on www.visualcv.com for free.

4. Set up a Paypal account for that occasional company you might come across that either utilizes paypal or uses checks and may utilize paypal to you upon your suggestion! *(I've had success in obtaining payment via paypal with small independent companies)*

CHAPTER 3. HOME OFFICE SET UP

Okay, so you've decided to give this working from home thing a shot? Below are listed in no particular order some things you need to consider before proceeding...

1. <u>Computer: desktop or laptop</u>.- *Laptops are nice, I've owned several of them however, your desktop will be your work horse.*

2. <u>Peripherals: desktop or laptop necessities</u>- *depending on your scenario most companies require some type headset for any CSR job. I suggest buying a couple of cheap ones from walmart, biglots and trying*

them out. I personally have had better success with 5.00 headsets than the 150.00 I purchased.

3. <u>Printer:</u> *stand-alone printer or multifunction device? Multi function printer wins hands down anyday! One that prints, scans and faxes.*

4. <u>Phone:</u> *landline or cellular or VOIP? Most virtual companies require "land-line" and some don't care..read their requirements! I've utilized all 3 to work from home.*

5. <u>Fax:</u> *refer to #3.*

6. <u>Furniture:</u> the right chair facing the right desk

7. <u>Networking/</u> <u>Internet:</u> *hardwired internet or wireless? Most virtual companies <u>require</u> "hardwired" again read their requirements.*

8. <u>Security:</u> *for the computer and for the office as a whole? Locks on doors! Locking file cabinets if required. Computer? Either make sure you're the only person using it or set up different User accounts on your PC so no one else has access to your work!*

9. <u>Environment:</u> *your office location - Must be a quiet location free from noise!*

CHAPTER 4. THE RESOURCES (THE GOLD)

- **<u>Work at Home Job Boards:</u>** www.RatRaceRebellion.com – This is the primary job board for work at home employment. Rat Race has been around for 11 years!!!!!! No signup necessary. IF you've never seen this site before, you will feel as though you have hit pay dirt! Happy browsing. The owner of the site has also written a book titled "WORK FROM HOME NOW"

- www.genuinejobs.com - This is another work from home job board that is updated regularly.

No signup necessary. You'll need to read each post carefully and do your research to find out if the job is still available as most employers will post an ad they placed on craigslist but never update the site owner that the job is no longer available.

- www.WorkatHomeMafia.com - great site, great layout, you don't have to join to read or post.

Work at Home Job Forums:

- www.WORKPLACELIKEHOME.com - This forum hasn't been around as long as the one below but I really like the layout. You must signup in order to view the posts and post comments. Lots of great info. Do your own due diligence, make your own decisions.

- www.WAHM.com - This site has been around a Loooong time..and has a TON of info. Info about different companies, the ladies or gents will post new jobs they find etc. When going to this site.... look to the left and click on "forums", inside there you'll want to search for jobs/ read the posts in the "telecommuting moms" folder.

Freelance Sites:

All of the sites below are freelance sites where Work on what you want, when you want and where you want to! The lifestyle of a freelancer is taking off and gives unparalleled job flexibility. Sign up and start bidding on jobs today!

- Freelancer.com
- Guru.com
- Odesk.com - Odesk is now Upwork.com

CHAPTER 5. ADDITIONAL TIPS

Other sites to search for telecommute employment are...

- Monster.com
- Careerbuilder.com
- Craigslist.org
- Allofcraigslist.com

2. **Boolean search terms:**

- work from home - IE: work from home appointment setter
- telecommute
- virtual - IE: virtual customer service
- contract
- contractor

3. **REPEAT AFTER ME**:

"Never pay to work from home. Never pay to work from home. **Never Pay to work from Home"**. Any job or company that requires up front money before you start work is "usually" considered to be some type of MLM scam and we' all know what those type of gigs are. IF you do pay, you do so at your own risk. Always search the forums to see if a job or company is legit. IF it's an all out scam, many, many people will voice their dismay... again use your own discernment. IF it sounds TOOOOOO good to be true, then it probably is.

4. How many Eggs are in your Basket?

Never put ALL your eggs in 1 basket!!!! (Unless it's a fortune 500 company and even then it's always good to have a back up!)

Find 2 or 3 jobs you can stick with working the minimum required hours because you never know when one job will fold leaving you empty handed.

ABOUT THE AUTHOR

AUTHOR NAME is BK Rich

Find out more at

amazon.com/author/bkrich

Or visit www.BKRich.com

OTHER BOOKS BY BK RICH
Coming Soon are:

What's Your Dinner Date Hiding?

How To Start A Virtual Call Center!

CAN I ASK A FAVOUR?

IF YOU ENJOYED THIS BOOK, FOUND IT USEFUL OR OTHERWISE THEN I'D REALLY APPRECIATE IT IF YOU WOULD POST A SHORT REVIEW ON AMAZON. I DO READ ALL THE REVIEWS PERSONALLY SO THAT I CAN CONTINUALLY WRITE WHAT PEOPLE ARE WANTING.

If you'd like to leave a review then please visit the link below:

http://amzn.to/1LqMJJz

Thanks for your support!